For my Family

Hares breath

Deep down
In the wild golden meadowland
Of my dream
Where the yellow sun blew
And brown-russet tall grasses
Rustled so gently and lulled the red cheek
children
Sleeping in their mother's nests
I was a great Hare

My long rear legs
Propelled me
With a power
Like no other
And I would leap
Over the bent grasses
As if flying
Over and over
And not a child
Did wake

The only sound
Was my breath

The horizon
Would tilt
As I leapt
My weight would crush the wild grassland
Push and fly
And push and fly

I would feel my ears
Stream behind me
The wind would rush
And the earth
Was singing songs to the revival

Try

Tiny Springtime birds
Need habitat
And are as daring
As they come
To collect beak-full loads
Of dried grasses
And broken twigs

They descend to the grass lawn
As I watch
From my chair
In our garden
And try not to move
Or breathe

"Don't look them in the eye"
Someone told me once
"Birds die if you look them in the eye"
So I avoid their darting gazes
And look silly
As I try not to move

Some might brag to hated neighbours
How they have nesting blue tits
And that the chicken was delicious
In the five star restaurant last Sunday
We did move to the suburbs
After all.

What need have they
To fear ?
Not of me
And I wish they knew
They were safe
Come and sit
In my hands

Yet now
I have mostly become
As they are
After I saw
What we are capable
Of doing

Gardening

I exclaimed
The wildflower garden
Was beautiful.
You seemed
Puzzled.
You thought
It was not.
"Nature does what it does. That's it"
Well. No. I thought.
That's not.

I thought of
the Gospel
From today-
That Stephen
and Barnabas
Were turned away
I will say why.
But in meantime
I thought
The wealthy
Ladies
The high priests turned to in their envy

Very much as
The Gladioli
That shooed Stephen away

And the Victorian's
High Anglican
With their habit
For naming things
And 'that is a weed
But that flower is not.'
You can believe,
Or you may not.

Yet seeds of love
Are scattered
For free
They grow up
Where they fall
Amidst this finery
Yet they are pretty
And can be happy and free

As the jealous
Flowers
Soon are cut
Left in a vase and then,   they rot.

You Know

Only you
Know
Just how to
Clean
Those long floppy ears
How to wet
Your paws
Turn your head
Sidewards and down
Pull one down
Then the other
In turn

Only you
Know
How to navigate
The tunnels
That keep you hidden
Where your young
Lie safe

When I was young
We bought a rabbit
That was kept in a cardboard box
In the dark
Back room
Of the local
Pet shop

We brought him home
And on our lawn
He didn't move
So unaccustomed
To freedom
Head down
Frightened

He did not know
How to clean
Either
So we washed him
Gently
And laughed
At how small he was
When wet

Only you know
That to leap,
Run,
Watch closely,
Give birth
And remain free
Is the only wisdom
On Earth.

Mouse House

It's obvious
Isn't it?
Mouse. House.
The rhymes
that delight the child
Yet offend
The 'sophisticated'
As they cringe
And laugh
Behind closed doors.

I see you scurry
And I know why
Yet I wish you ease
At least for a short time
I wonder
What you see of the world
From your fast low
Vantage point
It must be a blur
Like when I try
To photograph you

You must know
Your smallness
And the multitudes
Who would see you
Dead
For their own gain

I would very much
Like to build you
A mouse house
With a four poster bed
Velvet curtains
And high walls
Where you can languish
And be a Mouse King.

Difference

Yesterday
Was different
From today
In many ways

Today
Today is different

Yesterday
I managed to do things
I was in the garden
I moved pots
Planted flowers
Watered
And sat
And watched

The box
At the end
Is full of baby blue tits
They chirp loudly
Their parents
Non stop
Flying in
And out
And in again

I watch
From the bench
And one
Sits
On a branch prettily
Of the Magnolia tree

With a single swoop
Glides
The length of the garden
And enters
The tiny hole
Of the box
Such precision

Today
I am paying back
For yesterday

I lie on my bed
Surrounded by
'Ill things'
Half finished orange juice in a glass
A heart monitor
Tissues
My favourite toys from childhood
We all need some comfort

The windows are wide open
Today is very warm
And the curtains
Billow and blow
And I wish
They were sails
And that I might see
Diamond waves
And the shore

But I cannot
And there's a fly
Who is noisy
Chaotic
Stupid, even
As I watch
From my bed
It darts everywhere
It has no aim
No precision
Uses all its energy
Getting nowhere fast

In a few days
I may find it
Dead on a windowsill
Like the last.

Summer Snow

"It's incredible"

We exclaim
Each spring
Or at least I do

I always can't quite believe
A shrub
Be
So magnificent

I sent a photograph
Of it
To a friend
She exclaimed
"Those roses look like clouds!"
I'm glad I'm
Not the only one
And I explained
They were not roses
But hundreds of white spheres
Made up
Of thousands
Of tiny
Perfect white flowers

They overhang
The swinging bench.
To sit there
Is Heaven.
I planned it that way

Today,
The wind blows
And with each gust
The flowers fall
Like snow

The grass around the chair
Is covered white
With a green rectangle underneath.
The cushions
Have a deep cover of white
That slants up in one corner -
Just like when it snows
And the soil to one side
And the spade
Look like winter

Soon
It will be green
The flowers will fall
The snow melts away
Everything changes

This
Is what nature tells us
Year after year

Yet when
We must face the strain
Grow older
Children fly away
Watch the world
Grow faster
As we
Grow slow
Maybe
A part of us
Wishes
That the winter
Not
Melt into summer

Yet if it did not
Melt away
Today
Would not have been
Today

The Thing Is

What is?
You say
The thing
Today
Every day
It's something

I listen
Because that's
What I do
We all need
To be heard.
If I did not
Would you even be talking?

I say talking......

Yet so often,
More often
Than not
It's not so much
The song of the Blackbird
More

An angry starling

Your holiday
Yes…
Not enough sun loungers,
Poolside.
Every morning
Your alarm set
Earlier and earlier
Yet still,
Towels,
Every chair taken.
You used to say it
Was the Germans
I wonder now
If it's the Russians…

Perhaps
We've forgotten love
(What ever that has
To do with sun loungers)
But I recall
That the first
Shall be last…

No matter -

I watch birds
Again
Each has its nest
There's a squabble
As some tiny sparrows
Are chased
From the bird bath
By the pigeons

Stand your ground,
I thought,
No matter how small you are.
If you don't
There will soon
Be no place for you.
Yet they cheerfully find
Another place
To chirp
And play

It would be different
Perhaps
On holiday
Tipping a human
From a sun lounger?
May not be

Considered
As natural
As the cuckoo
Throwing out the eggs

We must keep watch.
As if
We did not,
Would anyone
Have been chased
From their land
Or killed?

Dianthus, the bee and Me

I sit down
To water the garden
We bought a folding chair
(I think mentioned elsewhere)
From a local Tesco
-other shops are available
Maybe even preferable
Yet for someone
Disabled
Often must needs

I digress

All the plants
Needed water
I sat happily
With the hose
Sprinkling refreshment
Until I reached
The Dianthus

More commonly known
As 'Bleeding Heart'
This one

Had strung up
Row upon row
Of the pretty heart shaped flowers
They are white, not pink
Like me
Anaemic
Perhaps?
Yet they show well
Against the grey fence

But what heart is white?

The water
Showers over
The pale green leaves
Dianthus shudders
And all of a sudden
Is swooped on
By three ginormous
Bumblebees

Now,
Don't get me wrong,
Last Summer
I spent the whole time
With the bees
As I grew
Pots of cornflowers
All from seed

I sat reclined
They didn't bother me
Although I first
Was frozen
The bumblebees came first
Later the honey bees
I saw the bees
And the bees saw me.

Yet these
Swooped noisily
Circling Dianthus
Then the water
And then me
As if to say
"Stop!"

Your plant needs water
I thought
But walked
To a different part of the garden
To come back

The roses have bloomed
The lilies are out
The climbers climbing

The Dahlias growing

I thought to try
Again
Under the cool shower
Dianthus shudders
Yet the three bees
Fly back
To protect her
I move on again.

Three times this
Same occurrence
Took place
That sunny
June afternoon
The others
The bees
Did not mind
Having water
And they were
Many and in full bloom

If they guard
What must be
So sweet to them
Like honey

They will kill
The thing they love
The white hearts
With no water
Will die

Starved of sustenance
The heart grows cold

Without blood
And love
It dies

Folded

I do need it
It must be lightweight
Foldable
Preferably colourful

I need it -
That chair
As the flowers
Need me.

Standing
To refresh them all
Is out of the question.
Who would think
Flowers be demanding?

I tell the smallest sweet pea
That no one thought would live but me
It stands as much chance
As the stronger ones

-I let the hose linger longer there

Standing tall
The Irises
Surely would rather be
In a pot
Wear a feather boa,
Yet they seem happy
With water and their lot,
As they dance
In the sun

Now the roses
Seem to cry to me
"We need water too!"
And despite their prickly spikes
Make up for this
With powdered blooms
-Old ladies
In tea rooms

Clematis tells me
As I sit nearby
She can now see
Over the garden fence
She has had such a climb

She thanks me
For the water
And we sit a while
And marvel
At how fast
Does pass the time

I move to by
The late bloomers
Plenty water here
I tell them they will have their time
And be patient
Waiting there

Then cry out now to me
The little pots
"We cannot drink
From earth, you put us here, now give us water
before we wither and die"
Each pot I move
My chair around
Wisteria is old and proud
Salvias have their saving graces
Pansies are
Little smiling faces.
I marvel at them all.

But now
I move the chair
To the wild place.
None of these I hear.
But prettiness reigns
And there is equality
And justice
For all who drift
From far away places
On the wind
Dandelions smile
Foxgloves stand proud
Buttercups
Corncockle teases the nearby Hydrangea

Cuckoo flowers so unlike the birds of that name
Daisies do nothing
But live simply and gently together
And I hope

People learn
To do the same

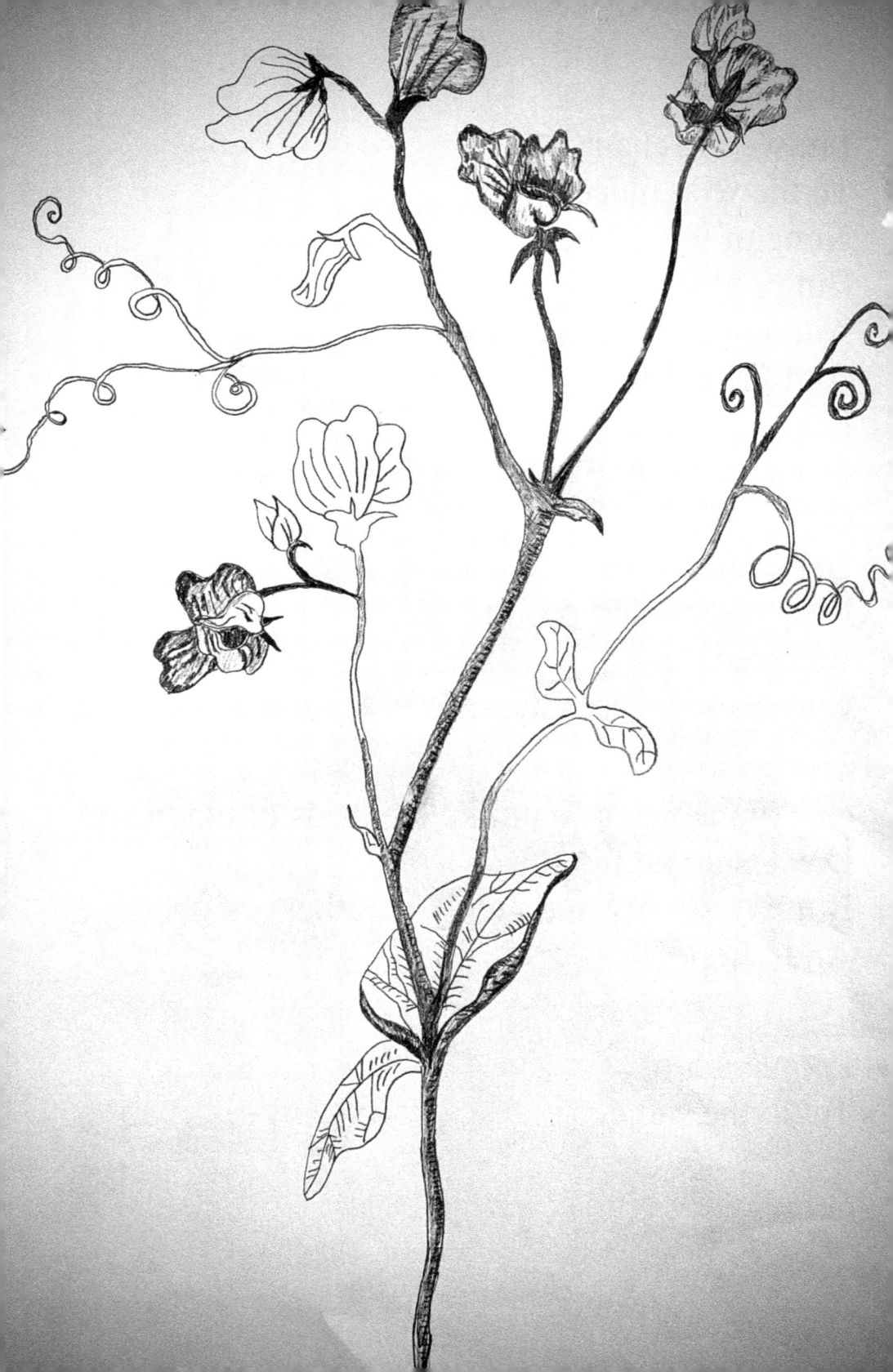

Solace

I saw
Their swift arrival
In the house
We had found
For them

It was hung
High enough
That cats
Could not jump
Yet the ferns
Gently surrounded
The tiny entrance

I heard
The tiny high strains
From within
As parents
Did not stop

On a wing
And a prayer
Surviving

Everyday
The voices
Got louder
Stronger

It was easy
To notice
When they
Flew the nest

It was quiet
The parents
Rested
Finding seeds among solace

Take comfort
They will
Return again

Just About

About to burst
Summer child
Sunday child
Full of Grace
Loving and giving
Beware the thorns
Below

When in the Winter
Of your Birth
Things lie hidden
Beneath cold fallen snow

Flowering crimson
Blood is spilt
Only in violence, birth
Or love

Flowers burst forth
In summer sun

Roses
Meant to speak
Of Love

You were
The envy
Of the Garden
Your sweet perfume
Aroused
Things forgotten

About to burst
Summer child
Sunday child
Full of Grace
Loving and giving
Beware the thorns
Below

When in the winter
Of your Birth
Things lie hidden
Deep beneath
Cold fallen snow

Then malice
Followed envy near
Spilled your blood
My sweetest dear
Leaving bereft
The Garden

Crimson born
Of love, passion or malice
Roses adorn the altar
As Priest
Does raise
The Chalice.

Tricky

It was a bit tricky
As I was at an angle
In my chair
But I saw the little squirrel
As it scampered
Down the palm tree
Nervously it tiptoed
And it
Saw me

Determined as it was
To enjoy
The fallen bird seed
It sat up on its hind legs
And sat down
For its tea

So sweet
It's tiny hands
It sat so still
Upon the grass
I'd like to have given
A tea set
And perhaps
A tiny gingham picnic cloth

Half an hour
In the sun
We enjoyed
Each other's company
The bushy tailed squirrel
The sweet peas
And me

Difference

It was a different day
Each one is
At least If you sit a while
Look around and think

The wind blew
The pages of the magazine
Anchored by
Coffee in a cup

Despite the gentle breeze
And the rumpled air
And the dependant leaves
Some heavy load remained

Somehow
The washing
Hanging To dry in melting sun
Looked solid

Despite its moving
The drapes
Were concrete
Or even bronze. Grecian

Underwear
Maybe after all
Having its impracticalities
Especially
In life's most meaningful
Or precarious moments.
And it's expensive

The coffee remaining
Spilt into the magazine

It made a head and shoulders
And I thought
How strange is the day.

2022

BUTTERFLY

Newcastle Poetry Fest

...ners

Poetry
Day

Feature
POEM

The air was clear
The air was clear
The moon was bright
But was I was lost
In my the letters lost
And
Over time

On 2nd April spring

Blackbird

She sat
On top of the fence
Near the end
Of our garden

The day was so hot
Humid, heavy
The damp laundry
In my arms weighed me down

She had her load too
A beak-full
Of what looked like
White berries
Whiter than my sheets

I've never been a mother
Seeking a gleaming home
I prefer the idea
Of a nest

She watched
As I hung up
The sheets
On the rotary line

She was not frightened
As it spun
And so I stopped
And her gaze met mine

I whistled gently to her
Through my tongue
She tipped her head
To the side

She seemed to want to stay
And so I stretched out my hand
But she didn't sit there
Yet didn't fly away

Yet she has her wings
I have only
My heavy body
And here it is
I must stay.

Still

You still are this?
Haven't you seen?
Can't you even begin
To understand

We all
Are borne of pain
If you could understand
How fast
The body fails
Falls apart
As leaves
After winter
Is done

And of the insults
Joy, tears, fears, suffering
Loves lost and found

We all
Are borne of pain
If you could understand
How fast
The body fails
Falls apart
As leaves
After winter
Is done

And of the insults
Joy, tears, fears, suffering
Loves lost and found

Pay credence then
To how brave
In the face of
Such a temporary life

Your heart
Then would break
And all the love
It holds
Would never
Be enough